essentials

Boost Your
Word Power

Time-saving books that teach specific skills to busy people, focusing on what really matters: the things that make a difference – the *essentials*.

Other books in the series include:

Business Letters that Work

Expand Your Vocabulary

Preparing a Marketing Plan

Leading Teams

Making the Most of Your Time

Solving Problems

Coaching People

Hiring People

Making Great Presentations

Writing Good Reports

The Ultimate Business Plan

Writing Business E-mails

For full details please send for a free copy of the latest catalogue. See back cover for address.

Boost Your Word Power

Brendan Hennessy

ESSENTIALS

Published in 2001 by
How To Books Ltd, 3 Newtec Place,
Magdalen Road, Oxford OX4 1RE, United Kingdom
Tel: (01865) 793806   Fax: (01865) 248780
e-mail: info@howtobooks.co.uk
www.howtobooks.co.uk

British Library Cataloguing in Publication Data.
A catalogue record for this book is available from
the British Library.

Edited by Julie Nelson
Cover design by Shireen Nathoo Design
Produced for How To Books by Deer Park Productions
Typeset by PDQ Typesetting, Newcastle-under-Lyme, Staffordshire
Printed and bound in Great Britain by Bell & Bain Ltd., Glasgow

NOTE: The material contained in this book is set out in good faith for
general guidance and no liability can be accepted for loss or expense
incurred as a result of relying in particular circumstances on
statements made in the book. Laws and regulations are complex
and liable to change, and readers should check the current position
with the relevant authorities before making personal arrangements.

ESSENTIALS *is an imprint of*
How To Books

Contents

Preface

To boost your word power, an increase in your active vocabulary is an obvious place to begin, so this book starts with that. But word power means, essentially, the ability to use your vocabulary with impact in speaking and writing, and the capacity to have some influence on people and events. Subsequent chapters, while continuing to reflect the joy that can be had from handling words, describe the techniques that will release that power.

In a world of increasing specialisation and ever speedier means of communication, word power keeps us abreast and involved. It obviously brings benefit to the student and increases the effectiveness of whatever we do to earn a living. But word power has a much wider value. It increases the richness of everyday life and makes our conversation more fruitful and interesting. It enables us to get more out of our thinking and reading, and deepens our understanding of the world around us. This book aims to appeal thus widely, showing how to get started on the fast track to eloquence and how to stay on it.

I am indebted to *Talk* magazine and Cristina Odone for permission to reproduce a paragraph from the article 'Bye, Society'; Jonathan Cape Ltd and Patrick Marnham for some lines from his book *So Far From God;* Penguin Books and V. S. Naipaul for some lines from the essay 'The Return of Eva Peron' in the book of that title; and to *The Guardian* and Tim Radford for the first paragraph of his article 'The Breakthrough that Changes Everything' in the issue of 26 June 2000. Quoted dictionary definitions are from the *Concise Oxford Dictionary*.

Brendan Hennessy

1 Increasing Your Vocabulary

*Words will yield power if they are gathered
in a creative way and constantly put to use.*

The point of building up your vocabulary is to increase your ability to assimilate ideas and to communicate effectively. Your curiosity and desire for self-expression, whatever your walk of life, will make it an enjoyable and rewarding task. This chapter gives you a strategy for turning the apparently passive, 'bookish' occupation of word collecting into a creative activity, which means keeping words under control and moving them from your passive (recognition) vocabulary to your active (words used) vocabulary.*

* The word power of your active vocabulary is released when you are in control.

When words take you over (and they are always trying to), you will say things you didn't mean, and mean things you didn't say.

You will increase your vocabulary by:

1. gathering purposefully

2. raiding the dictionaries

3. recognising word forms and functions

4. playing word games.

Is this you?

As a civil servant I have to explain the policies of my department to new recruits on occasion, both in writing and speaking. This is the only part of my job which I don't perform well. • I know what Hamlet meant when he said: 'My words fly up, my thoughts remain below;/ Words without thoughts never to heaven go.' • I use 10 words instead of one, because the right one doesn't come to me. • I read a lot and have a lot of words but they are as often in control of me as I am in control of them. I need some kind of system that will help me to show who's in charge. • I wince when I hear George W. Bush come out with 'hostage' when he means *hostile*, and 'subliminable' for *subliminal*, because that's the sort of thing I do myself and it can be very embarrassing.

Gathering purposefully

To ensure that adding to your vocabulary will add to your word power, follow this plan of action:

~ **Collect words you are likely to use.** Take them from various sources: from your experience of life, from books, newspapers and magazines and from other media, from computer programs and from listening to the radio, lectures, talks and conversations.

~ **Guess a word's meaning from the context.** Use any clues to the meaning, such as your recognition of word elements. Then check your guess against the dictionary definition. Suppose you meet *homomorphic* as an unfamiliar word. You can recall, perhaps, that *homogeneous* means: parts all of the same kind, and that *amorphous* means: no clearly defined form.

You can then deduce that *homomorphic* means: of the same or similar form.

~ **Record your words** in a notebook and on cards. Collect them in a notebook wherever you are, and transfer them to 5″ by 3″ cards, with meanings added when you have access to your dictionary. Arrange the cards in alphabetical order in catalogue boxes. Recording words in the way illustrated (see Fig. 1) helps to fix them in the mind.

~ **Make regular memory checks**. Cover up everything on the front of the card except the word and see if you can recall all the information there, and perhaps the sample sentences on the back as well. Put ticks on the corners of front and back when you feel you can recall enough. Test yourself with your cards periodically. When a card has two or three ticks on both corners, put it in another box labelled 'Mastered'.

FRONT

glutton, n.

an excessively greedy eater → *a person who is very fond of something* → `he is a glutton for poetry`

gluttonize (also -ise), v.
gluttonous, adj, gluttonously, adv.
origin: ME: from OFr gluton, *from L.* glutto *(n-), rel to* gluttire, *to swallow,* gluttus, *greedy and* gula, *throat*

BACK

`The glutton cannot pass a restaurant without studying the menu and saying he is hungry.`

`He is a glutton for punishment, always ready to do the difficult tasks.`

Fig. 1. Word card.
ME: Middle English, OFr: Old French, L: Latin

Raiding the dictionaries

At home you will need at least one of the medium sized dictionaries such as the *Concise Oxford* or *Chambers*. Check what help they give with language matters other than meanings, such as usage, word elements (word formation), etymology (origins and development of words), idiomatic phrases, foreign phrases. There are specialised dictionaries on these and many other aspects (aphorisms, fables, rhymes, slang) and you may want to add one or two of these to your collection. Find out what your local reference library has on its shelves. If you have a computer there are various word programs that can save you shelf space.

Note context influences

Words can vary greatly in meaning according to context. Context may involve such aspects as **field**, **subject area**, **register**, **connotation**, **collocation**, **tone** and **region**. Check the ways in which dictionaries deal with such aspects before making a choice. These terms are discussed further in Chapters 5 and 6.

Consult dictionaries of synonyms

Some dictionaries include a section for synonyms or for both synonyms and antonyms under the headwords. If yours doesn't you will also need a thesaurus (dictionary of synonyms). Compare the classic *Roget's Thesaurus*, arranged by concepts, with the more recent ones, arranged alphabetically in dictionary form.

Consult a thesaurus to find the *precise* word for what you mean. The adjective escapes you, perhaps, that means: 'understood only by a select group of people'. You know the word *abstruse,* but that will not quite do. You look under the headword *abstruse* in *The New Collins Thesaurus*. You find: 'abstract, arcane, complex, dark, deep, enigmatic, esoteric, hidden, incomprehensible, mysterious, mystical, obscure, occult, perplexing, profound, puzzling, recondite, subtle, unfathomable, vague'. You read through them all, though you have now found the word you want: *esoteric.*

Follow the consensus on meanings

You may want to fight against shifts in meaning. It's a pity, perhaps, to use *disinterested* to mean 'uninterested', as is now accepted, and to lose that fine distinction that the meaning 'unbiased' confers. But when you trace *disinterested* back to its origin in the eighteenth century you find that it then meant *uninterested*. And there is grammatical evidence to support that meaning. Remember that dictionaries do not *prescribe*; they *describe* the language used at a particular time.

In the seventeenth century *indifferent* meant 'impartial' and *awful* meant 'awe-inspiring'. In the eighteenth century *disgusting* meant 'not in good taste'. Reading the literature of past centuries we need to be aware of such changes, and we need to be alert to day-by-day changes in the present. Meanings can become weakened (*adore, besotted, fabulous*), and informal registers (*cool, wicked*) may take over or drop out.

The challenge may be to find other ways of saying what the words used to say unequivocally, and you should accept the challenge.

Thus dictionaries are a little out of date as soon as they are printed, and dictionary makers are constantly updating for their next edition, noting (in conversation, in the media and other sources) shifts in meaning and the appearance of new words. Dictionaries devoted to new words are now produced regularly, so fast do they need to cope with the advance of sciences and new technologies.

Recognising word forms and functions

The chief aim of raiding word stores and recording your findings is to recognise and note the functions of:

~ word origins

~ distinct meanings

~ idiomatic phrases

~ word elements.

Word origins

Knowing the origins of a core word can help you to recognise its various appearances. Look up the words *gregarious* and *egregious* in your dictionary and see the effects of the affixes on the core meaning of *flock* (Latin *grex, gregis*).

For historical reasons – early invasions, creation of an empire, an economy based on trade – the language of our islands has borrowed more than most from others. Modern English is dated from about 1500. The origins listed in the dictionary include, as well as all the European languages, Anglo-Saxon or Old English (which dates to around 1150), Middle English (to 1500), Latin, Greek (both ancient and modern), Hebrew, Arabic, Turkish and Chinese. Examples are, respectively, *crafty*, *passage* (from Old French via Latin), *ultimatum*, *stigma*, *shibboleth*, *algebra*, *yoghurt*, *typhoon*.

Many foreign words and phrases borrowed are well known, though not yet fully naturalised in English. They tend to be printed in roman font, as in this paragraph, rather than in italics. Latin gives us: 'ad hoc' and 'prima facie', French: 'cause célèbre' and 'raison d'être'; German: 'Bildungsroman', a novel dealing with one person's early life and development, and 'schadenfreude', pleasure derived from another's misfortune.

Some keep their accents, some don't. 'Débâcle' is seen like that, and also like this — 'debacle'. German words may or may not lose their initial capitals (see the contrasting examples above). Follow the usage of your chosen dictionary.

Lesser known borrowings, called **foreignisms**, are italicised. Here are some examples: the French *une lapalissade* ('a statement of the obvious'), the Italian *ma non troppo* ('but not excessive'), the Spanish *mañana* ('in the indefinite future', literally 'tomorrow'), the Portuguese *auto-da-fé* (the burning of a heretic by the Spanish Inquisition, literally 'act of the faith'), and the German *Gastarbeiter* (a person with temporary permission to work in another country, especially in Germany).

Distinct meanings

English is notable for the several distinct meanings (*polysemy*) that many words have. The *Concise Oxford Dictionary* gives seven meanings for *charge* as a verb: charge as a price, accuse, entrust with a task, store electric energy, load a container such as a gun, rush forward in attack, and (heraldry) place a charge on. These are followed by eight meanings as a noun.

Idiomatic phrases

Many are worth recording, especially the more unusual ones made by linking common verbs (*bring, cut, get, put, see,* etc.) with prepositions. Pity the foreign student of English who has to *get his head round* the wealth of meanings.

Word elements

There are four elements: *core words (roots* or *bodies), prefixes* (affixes starting words), *suffixes (*affixes ending words) and *combining forms* (affixes specifically used to form new words). The word *interchangeable* contains the root *change*, the prefix *-inter* and the suffix *-able*. The combining form *pseudo-* gives us such words as *pseudo-science.*

Affixes

Affixes add flexibility to the resources of English and their meanings are separately listed among the headwords of a good dictionary. Among the commonest affixes, which number over a hundred, are *a-*, *anti-*, *bi-*, *-circum*, *com-*, *contra-*, *de-*, *in-*, *dis-*, *-ment*, *-ness*, *pre-*, *re-*, *-ion*. Note that some prefixes change in spelling to adapt to the following sound: *com*mute (for *con-*), *im*minent (for *in-*).

Watch out for variations in the basic meaning of some prefixes. *Dis-* can mean negation (*displeasure*), reversal *(disclaim)*, or removal (*disrobe*). Similar-looking prefixes can vary in meaning. *Hypo-* means 'under, below normal' (*hypodermic* means 'underneath the skin'); but *hyper-* means 'over, beyond, above' (as in *hyperactive*).

Suffixes have a more practical and predictable function: the noun *region* adds *-al* to become an adjective, the noun *myopia* turns into *myopic*. The adjective *real* becomes *realistic* and can turn into the adverb *realistically*.

Combining forms

These are word parts that function as prefixes or suffixes: for example, *anthrop-*, human being (from the Greek *anthropos*), combines with *-ology* (sometimes *-logy*, also originally from the Greek), the study of. You can kill a lot of people by adding *-cide* to them (*fratricide*, *regicide*, and so on).

The more 'wordlike' combining forms such as *psych-* (mind) and *-phobia* (fear of) have spawned a vast number of new words. *Phobia*, as well as having a word life of its own, has contributed to some astonishing-sounding problems (*kakorrhaphiaphobia* is the fear of failure) as well as the more obvious ones (*telephonophobia*). *Cyber-*, from the Greek *kubernetes*, steersman, has been used since the 1940s for information technology (IT) coinages, and the government's online health service has produced *cyberchondriac*.

Compounds

English is equally resourceful in the way two words can come together in one, the connection between them becoming familiar and obviating wordy explanation: *aircraft*, *dreamland*, *flashpoint*, *horseplay*, *neckcloth*. Hyphenated examples are *Afro-Caribbean*, *double-entry*, *kerb-crawling*, *shop-soiled*.

'Conversions'

As inflections were lost in Modern English, Shakespeare delighted his word-hungry contemporaries with the way he exploited parts of speech. He turned nouns into verbs ('curtained sleep'), into adjectives ('salad days'), adjectives into verbs ('better the instruction'), a conjunction into both verb and noun ('but me no buts'), and so on. Such a long-established practice is hardly noticed now: we *film* it or *fax* it, we say he *lectured* to the company, or that he talked with a *Lancashire* accent.

Playing word games

English lends itself to word play and word games, to having fun with words. That fun can have serious literary intent behind it: from Chaucer, through Shakespeare and James Joyce, to today's poets, novelists and dramatists, breaking the rules can produce delightfully rewarding effects. Puns, riddles, repartee, deviant grammar and punctuation are productive devices for the writer who uses wit to keep readers awake and stimulated.*

Word play is a way of adding entertainment to your vocabulary-building activity. It keeps alive the fascination of words (as children constantly remind us). **Word games** are more structured devices, though the dividing line is not distinct. Crossword puzzles and Scrabble are played at vastly different levels of erudition. Try devising a few *acrostics*, *anagrams* and *palindromes*. Tony Augard has produced several fascinating collections of word games for the Oxford University Press.

* *Experiment with word play and you'll find that the better you know the rules the more convincing will be your breaking of them.*

Practice

Check your answers to the following exercises against the key on page 114. Check dictionaries after that if you want to include any of the words on cards.

1. Select the word or phrase that best defines the word in italics:

   (a) a *vicarious* pleasure: sinful, enjoyed by vicars, experienced indirectly

   (b) a *notorious* gambler: well known, famous for something bad, noteworthy

   (c) a *lapidary* writing style: concise, careless, dense

   (d) an *acrimonious* discussion: full of irony, fruitful, bitter

   (e) the *ostensible* motive: obvious, apparently true, apparently untrue

2. Find the words that match the definitions:

   (a) a lover and collector of books

   (b) firmly established (habit, procedure)

   (c) outside the earth or its atmosphere

(d) outside a country's territory

(e) a fine detail or distinction, a detail of etiquette

3. Since words can have more than one meaning, one word can be a synonym for more than one other word. Find one synonym for both words in these pairs:

(1} troupe, ensemble

(2) humorous, playful

(3) dismember, cut to pieces

(4) comparison, correspondence

(5) deluded, ill-advised

4. Give five different meanings for the noun *round*.

5. Rearrange the following letters to make a word: *pnlleeeesssss*.

6. Sort out the confusables.
A word may be confused with another word if the pair are *homonyms* (spell the same) or *homophones* (sound the same), or *distinguishables* (are similar in sound or

meaning and needing to be distinguished).

Example: Distinguish between *immanent* and *imminent*.
Immanent means 'existing or operating within'
Imminent means 'about to happen'.

Distinguish between:

(a) *catholic* and *Catholic*
(b) *eligible* and *illegible*
(c) *cultured* and *cultivated*
(d) *sestet* and *sextet*
(e) *allusion* and *illusion*
(f) *credible* and *credulous*
(g) *affect* and *effect* (verbs)
(h) *imply* and *infer* (but the distinction is being eroded)
(i) *pendant* and *pendent*
(j) *gourmand* and *gourmet*

2 Making Words Work in Teams

The force in words is created by the context. Make them collaborate with those around them.

Is this you?

Although I enjoy lively discussions with my friends, with other people I'm either tongue-tied or pompous. • Close friends find my letters interesting, but I spend a lot of time waffling about, I'm looking for the right way to say things and not finding them if you get what I mean when I'm writing to other people. I never come straight out with it in other words, I tend to say 'one feels a mistake has been made' rather than 'you have made a mistake'. • In some of my college subjects I have to study texts that are full of jargon and I find it hard to explain things in my own words and come to my own conclusions.*

* *Style is the man himself, as the Frenchman said (he meant women as well). Increasing skill with language boosts your confidence and with it your ability to communicate.*

What team power means

The American writer Mark Twain wrote to a friend: 'I would have written a shorter letter but I didn't have time.' Most good pieces of writing have been through several drafts, and much of the rewriting has involved **reducing**: removing the irrelevant and the verbiage, tightening up.

The power unit is the sentence, where the power of your words is released. To avoid monotony, sentence lengths and structures must be varied. The modern sentence, however, works best when it is lean and muscular, clear and concise. That means, as far as possible, an average length of 15 to 20 words.

The whole of the power unit sentence, however, must be greater than the sum of its words, and the whole of the paragraph greater than the sum of its sentences, and the whole of your piece greater than the sum of the paragraphs.

You can make words work in teams by:

1. planning and connecting

2. keeping to the subject and viewpoint

3. creating a network of references

4. linking and signposting.

Planning and connecting

Before you write a piece of any length, or give a speech, do any necessary preparation (research) and planning. Produce an outline if necessary. Ask yourself:

~ Have I got something to say?

~ Is there a unified theme or point of view? (If there is a title, it should reflect this.)

~ Who am I talking to?

~ What effect am I aiming at? Informing? Persuading? Making them laugh? Making them cry? Moving them to action?

~ What is the best order?

Planning what you want to say, whether in your head or in a written outline, will help you to achieve unity and coherence, to keep to the point. You may prefer to sail in with a first draft, see what you've got, and then rearrange it.

Make the connections clearly between one paragraph and the next and between one sentence and the next. Your audience should be carried smoothly through the journey, hardly aware of the changes in direction and gear changes.

Keeping to the subject and viewpoint

If you are arguing, for example, that more financial help should be given to university students, you may want to include a note on how pensioners could be helped to acquire computer literacy, but discussing a proposal that they should get free milk may well need another occasion.

When what you have to say is both long and complex, there is an even greater need to help the audience to see the connections by preparing them with an introduction and by summing up your viewpoint or conclusion in the ending.

Check that each paragraph makes it clear what the connection is between the aspect covered and the subject of the whole. Grammatically speaking, check that the subjects of the sentences of a paragraph don't change too often. There should be clearly one main topic, though it isn't always expressed in a 'topic sentence'.

Creating a network of references

There are three kinds of references to consider: *key terms and ideas*, *referential words* and *repeated grammatical patterns*.

Key terms and ideas

Read for a second time any piece of factual writing without dialogue containing several paragraphs and underline the key terms and ideas that are repeated. You may be surprised to discover how often they're repeated, since it was done in such a way that you hadn't noticed the first time. Here is one paragraph I have extracted from an article by Cristina Odone in the April 2000 issue of the magazine *Talk*, about Italian socialites becoming nuns. Terms related to the church are italicised, those related to the aristocracy are in bold type:

In Italy, *church* and **aristocracy** have long been linked. Several *popes* have long been scions of the **nobility** – de Medici, Orsini, Pallavicini, Farnese, Della Chiesa. By the 1500s, for **patrician** women the *nunnery* served as the only respectable alternative to marriage; when a daughter's **dowry** was considerably lower than that demanded by prospective spouses, it was an option fathers favoured. Throughout the Renaissance, more than one third of the daughters of the Italian **aristocracy** entered the *convent*, some willingly. Today **titled** families still retain *religious* traditions that have fallen from favour among the rest of **society**: *Mass* on *holy days* and on Sunday, *church* schools for children, family *pilgrimages* to *Lourdes* and other *shrines*.

Note how the first (topic) sentence sums up

the whole paragraph. Such a sentence generally works best at the beginning or end of a paragraph. There are other chains of related terms to complete the network: *fathers*, *daughters*, *families* and *long, throughout the Renaissance* and *today*.

Referential words

If key terms are not so much in focus, such referential words as the definite article *(the,* various lines) and pronouns (*that,* lines 8 and 15 and *it,* line 9) are more in evidence, plus comparatives ('the bigger', 'the smaller', 'the former', 'the latter', 'similar'...).

Repeated grammatical patterns

Because the sentences beginning *Throughout the Renaissance...* and *Today...* have the same grammatical pattern, they are in parallel and echo each other to underline the contrast between the two periods of time. Similar patterns are: 'in some situations...in others...', 'to the south...to the east...', 'it is obvious that...it is less obvious that...'*

* Lists of statements or questions, especially if numbered or bullet-pointed, should be in parallel.

Linking and signposting

Television and computers have encouraged communication by sound bites; linear-logical development of ideas is neglected; and students' essays are more disjointed than they used to be. **Linking words** – the conjunctions *and*, *but* and *so* (as well as the relative pronouns *which*, *that*, *who*, *whose*) – deserve to get in the team more often, and so do the longer linking words and phrases, especially when changing gear, as at the start of paragraphs. They include *furthermore*, *what is more*, *however*, *nevertheless*, *therefore*, *consequently*, *for example*, *to put these problems into perspective*. The longer phrases can serve to give the audience a breathing space.

You can balance your connectives, as on a signpost, between where you've come from and where you're going. This is particularly useful halfway through a piece when you want to make sure your audience is still with you. You may say, for example, in so many words, that the foregoing has covered *that*; what follows will cover *this*. For example: '*Not only* did they . . . *but* they *also* . . . and similar pairs of phrases.

Connectives tend to be lacking in first drafts, especially when not planned beforehand, because to the writer the connections are obvious. Look for the gaps when editing, that is, when reading your draft with the eyes and ears of an audience.*

Practice

1. The following passage is wordy and lacks connectives. Reduce it by a half, but supply connectives. Avoid the changes of subject. Check your effort with the key on page 117.

A patient with a fairly unusual disease was in the habit of accessing the internet and he discovered a treatment for his disease which was much better than and more effective than the treatment he had been getting from his doctor, which was not working very well at all. He lost all faith in his doctor. His doctor, as it happened, had had very little experience with the

* The connectives should scarcely be noticeable in your final draft.

particular disease. It isn't possible for GPs to keep absolutely up to date with all the latest research connected with all the various illnesses they happen to be dealing with at any particular moment. There is more to medicine than facts. The patient continued to treat himself with the help of the internet and came to a sad end. Another disease was contracted and there grew in him an obsession to find out all he could from the internet about it. This time among the numerous facts was a fair amount of what can only be described as misleading information, and to cut a long story short he took doses of two drugs which should not be taken together. You need plenty of knowledge and judgement to assess the value of information and this time the internet let him down badly, to put it mildly, because unfortunately he died. (217 words).

2. Using appropriate connections and reordering as necessary, rewrite the following sentences in the form of a paragraph.

Some people say England was a class-ridden country.

It was undoubtedly full of snobbery and privilege.

The rulers were dull and unimaginative.

The country has emotional unity.

The inhabitants tend to feel alike and act together at times of crisis.

During the two world wars the people felt united.

Some people say that the country is no longer class-ridden.

Some people say that it is just as class-ridden as it always was.

3 Aiming to be Concise

A sentence should be as simple and direct as its subject allows. Every word must count.

Is this you?

At present I'm studying Computer Science, although I'm not sure if it's the right thing for me, if that's the way to put it. At the end of the day everybody's going to be using computers anyway so that part of my education won't be wasted will it? Working long hours at the screen has not helped me to speak better or write better – I couldn't say exactly why to tell you the honest truth, it seems to be using different parts of the brain. It's good for encouraging lateral thinking in my case, at least I think it is, but I find that planning what I want to write or say in a logical pattern is very difficult, I mean I kind of seize up with the tedium of it, so I write down what comes into my head with the idea of rewriting it if absolutely necessary because

I know that's what you're supposed to do. The trouble is it always seems OK to me.*

Thinking clearly

The above writer's redundant words and phrases are evidence that content and audience have not been clearly determined. There's nothing wrong with writing first drafts in this way as long as the result doesn't 'seem OK to you' and as long as you put yourself in the reader's place and **edit**. Which generally means **cut**.

Uncertainty in your statements makes for uncertain and reluctant readers. The more you have struggled to think things out and come to a clear point of view, and the more trouble you have taken to communicate as clearly and as concisely as the subject allows, the easier you are making it for the reader.

You can aim to be concise by:

1. editing for relevance

2. weeding out the modifiers

3. removing other verbiage.

*Unless we are aiming to communicate them to others, we must prevent the uncertainties in our lives from making what we have to say unclear.

Editing for relevance

You may have spent much time on researching and writing a piece, and find it hard to cut. Put your piece away for a day or two so that you can assess it more objectively. You may need an editor other than yourself to help.

You may have boiled down the contents of a long book on ancient Egyptian tombs (a particular interest of yours perhaps) to make two paragraphs in an essay on Tourism in North Africa. The material, however, may deserve only one paragraph. Or just one or two sentences. Or it may have to go. It depends on how long the piece is and who it is aimed at.

That long quote from Shakespeare may suggest that you're well-read, that anecdote out of personal experience may hint at an interesting personality, that joke may indicate a sharp sense of humour. But do they earn their places?*

Digression is self-indulgence.

Editing, however, should be done with a scalpel rather than a scythe, provided enough care has gone into the writing. Keep your early drafts, because in the course of rewriting you may find that previously rejected or doubtful bits make stronger claims for inclusion.

Weeding out the modifiers

More straightforward generally than the above surgery is the removal of unnecessary words.*

Unnecessary adverbs can hamper a verb's performance

'*Basically*, I prefer Thackeray to Dickens' and '*Predictably*, she was in one of her fault-finding moods' betray with those adverbs a desire to be considered thoughtful: a second thought would have removed them. Adverbial phrases after a verb, as in 'the teacher frowned *with irritation*' often betray a lack of faith in your verb. Leave the phrase out, or find a stronger verb. *Scowled*? *Glowered*?

In such phrases as '*absolutely* necessary', '*vitally* important', '*quite* perfect', *totally*

* *The verb, the engine of the sentence, has to be kept clean and strong.*

honest', '*actually quite* interesting', the adverbs are unnecessary. The aim is to intensify the meaning, but they reduce the impact.

Reject superfluous modifiers

Modifiers should earn their place by making what you say more precise. Consider the following adjective-noun pairs.

the honest truth
a barefaced lie
the true facts
a grave emergency
an acute crisis
the prerequisite conditions
in-depth research
under active consideration
a final conclusion.

Rather than add to the nouns the adjectives here cast doubt on the values of the nouns and create suspicion. The adjectives were clinging on when the nouns were reached for. Avoid adjectives that aim to add intensity or emphasis, and look for those that are factual, or denote kind, as in the following list:

a damaging lie
the hidden facts
the unacceptable conditions
historical research
a lamentable conclusion.

Adjectives tend to be lined up in support when the noun lacks accuracy or strength. Find the more precise noun. For example:

a *powerful, rushing stream* is a *torrent*
the *main character* is the *protagonist*
a *flattering, toadying hanger-on* is a *sycophant*
a *sheer drop* is a *precipice*.

Use a thesaurus when you know that the noun you want has escaped you. Or verb:

to *express complete disapproval of* is to *condemn*.

Adverbs are often used unnecessarily. Among the common interlopers are *definitely* ('I will definitely go there'), *really* ('he really did feel sorry'), *unduly* (the group were unduly harassed'), *very* ('a very desirable outcome' and, worse, 'a very real danger'), and *relatively*

(relatively few students failed' – relative to what?)

Use meaningful modifiers

There are, of course, meaningful modifiers that can say a lot in the right places, and the best journalism is a good place to find them.

Recent novel reviews had the phrases: '*ranting, amorphous, cut-up-and-paste* style' and '*edgy, sharp and genuinely shocking*'. A film review: 'The backgrounds are *painstakingly* done, with the Dresden set-piece an *unexpectedly impressive* wasteland of rubble and smoke.' A review of Shakespeare's *Richard III*: '*gloved, mis-shaped* arm, *heavy* limp, and *crew-cut* head sticking *tortoise-like* out of a *stooped, hunchbacked* body'.

Here the modifiers justify their space, summing up vividly.

Removing other verbiage

There are two main kinds of verbiage, or wordiness: circumlocution and tautology.

Circumlocution

This means 'walking round the subject', using many words where few will do, and is at work here: 'He had to learn to be content with the circumstances of his life as they were and avoid constantly dreaming about what they would be if they were perfect.'
Rewrite: 'He had to learn to be content with his actual life rather than dream about the ideal.'

Wordy phrases commonly replacing single words include 'as a result of the fact that' (*because*), and phrases containing the words 'condition', 'character', 'nature', 'problem' and 'question'. For 'the ground was in a soggy condition', write 'the ground was soggy'.

Prepositions and conjunctions have spawned unnecessary extensions. *For* is better than 'for the purpose of', *except* is better than 'with the exception of', *about* is better than 'in the neighbourhood of'.

Long words in fashion that rarely improve on the short alternative include 'facilitate' (*ease*), 'implement' (*do*), 'numerous' (*many*), and 'parsimonious' (*mean*).

Tautology

This is the unnecessary repetition within a statement of the same thing in different words.

Example: 'The ships disappeared from sight after continuing to fire broadside after broadside into the town.'

Rewrite: 'The ships disappeared after firing many broadsides into the town.'

Practice

1. Rewrite the following sentences to make them more concise and clearer.

   (a) The manager of the housing department said that he would use the computer to produce an updated report on repairs required at the council meeting on Thursday.

   (b) The reaction of the audience to the orchestra's performance was one of loud appreciation.

   (c) The film we saw was not the sort that holds my attention for long.

(d) The company was upgrading its customer complaints procedures by means of providing training for staff in specially designed courses.

2. Rewrite the **Is this you?** section on page 41 (167 words) in 70–75 words, imagining you are the student, with readers clearly in mind.

4 Crafting the Forceful Sentence

Sentences must have variety, with well-chosen verbs, and an order that creates rhythm and the right emphases.

Is this you?

I drafted the following letter:

Dear Resident

As Consultation Officer for the West Bingleton Borough Council Housing Department site visits by members of your District Panel members and Housing Department Officers have to be arranged by me in respect of authors of completed application forms presenting Environmental Improvement Scheme Proposals relating to their respective sites. As the author of a completed application form I am writing to you since suggested dates for site visits at 10 a.m. have to be confirmed as convenient by the applying residents concerned, so a form is enclosed wherein the said residents can indicate confirmation of the suitability of those times.

My boss suggested the following rewrite, as a combined letter/form:

With reference to your proposal, would you please confirm by ticking the box that (date) would be convenient for site visits by District Panel members and Housing Department Officers? If the time is not convenient, would you please tick boxes against the list of dates below?

Plain English

Since its founding in 1979 the Plain English Campaign has had much success in persuading all kinds of organisations to replace gobbledygook with clear, readable English. The word *gobbledygook* originated in the USA in the 1940s and means 'meaningless or unintelligible language, especially when over-technical or pompous'. Its main characteristics are over-use of abstract nouns, lack of vigorous verbs, verbiage, faulty grammar and lack of a sense of the reader's needs.

You can craft the forceful sentence by:

1. putting the vigour into the verb

2. keeping words in their places

3. developing an ear for rhythm.

Putting the vigour into the verb

The most easily understood word order for an English sentence is: grammatical subject, followed by predicate (what is said about the subject), which must contain a finite verb. For example: 'Jesus wept.' If the verb needs an object that comes next: 'John bought a bike.'

If you have written a long and unclear sentence, you can often unravel it by asking yourself what the subject is and what the predicate is. You can reduce it by ordering it like 'John bought a bike', bringing subject and verb nearer the beginning. To repeat, sentences must vary. But a text that too often separates subject from verb, and too often places the pair towards the end of sentence, is hard to read.

Use active verbs rather than nouns

'The removal of the bandages by the nurse should have taken place before the arrival on the wards of the registrar' is 21 words and is better as 'the nurse should have removed the bandages before the registrar arrived on the wards', which is 14 words.

You sound more important (to yourself) if you say 'made reference to' instead of 'referred to' and 'results in the satisfaction of' instead of 'satisfies', but it is the single verbs that are superior.

Reading short, simple and honest sentences can win you over, taking you to where the author is. Patrick Marnham achieves this in his book about Central America, *So Far From God*. Here he is in Plaza Morazan, Tegucigalpa, Honduras, watching a five-year-old boy and his young sister walking with their mother:

He was walking backwards down the centre of the square, gazing up at his mother who followed behind. Round his neck was a loop of string, the end of which his mother held tightly. His mother was blind. She carried a heavy wooden box under one arm and there was an even smaller child, a girl, clinging to her skirts and walking silently behind her. In the mother's other hand she also carried a thick staff. On and on bawled the boy. His face as he retreated was raised to his mother's, and the string was taut.

Prefer active verbs to passive

Active verbs push the sentences forward. 'The form must be returned to this office' is better expressed as 'Please return the form to us', even if you're in the army. Even less vigorous is the impersonal passive: 'It is regretted that the repairs will not be completed within the period originally designated' means (it is to be hoped) 'We regret that we shall not complete the repairs as soon as we expected.'

Putting bloodless words into the passive, preceded by cloudy abstract nouns, tells the

reader you've got something to hide.
'Collateral counterforce damage of second
strike capability has been carried out' means
they killed many, many people. 'Ethnic
cleansing' and 'pacification' are among other
abstract words employed as euphemisms.

Prefer to be positive
Usually 'he failed' is preferable to 'he didn't
succeed', 'I admit it' to 'I don't deny it'.
Readers pick up a positive statement more
quickly than a negative one.

Avoid mixing a **negative** with an **implied
negative**. Implied negatives such as 'avert'
and 'unless' can cause trouble. Prefer 'always
keep your eyes open' to 'never avert your
eyes from'. 'Unless you have a good excuse
you will not be allowed to attend' is better as
'You will be allowed to attend only if you
have a good excuse'.

Unnecessary caution may be caused by lack
of confidence or lack of vocabulary or a
combination of both, and results in the
usually redundant 'it seems that . . .', 'I rather
think that . . .', 'it is within the realms of
possibility', and suchlike.

Keeping words in their places

This means keep words related to the subject, or to the verb, or object or indirect object, as near as possible to those elements. The following sentence lets the words climb over each other looking for their rightful places:

> The football team, to use the facilities in a nearby city of a sports club in the suburbs, travelled there for intensive training sessions every Thursday evening.

It is slowed down by that middle, and is clogged up with prepositions. Keep subject and main verb together, as a general rule. For example:

> The football team travelled every Thursday evening to a nearby city's suburbs to train intensively at a sports club.

Look again at the Marnham extract above and note how he varies the sentence structures while keeping the subjects and predicates clear. Then use the above sentence to practise varying a sentence's structure, noticing how the emphasis changes. Keeping related parts together, complete these:

'By travelling to the suburbs...'
'In the suburbs of...'
'To use the facilities of...'

Misplacing a word can lead to ambiguity. 'The chairman of the amateur theatre society said he expected a few members were going to pair off and get married at the annual general meeting yesterday' is clearer as: 'At the annual general meeting of the amateur theatre society yesterday the chairman said he expected a few members were going to pair off and get married.' Did you notice the misplaced phrase in the last sentence of the **'Is this you?'** section on page 51?

Developing an ear for rhythm

Without rhythm, a sentence, however well chosen the words, from however well stocked a vocabulary, can be lifeless on the page. The ancient oral storyteller knew that rhythm plus sound gave a music to his words that made them memorable. The first writers were poets.

Rhythm is dictated by the stresses in the words, the shifts from short words to long, the punctuated pauses, the shifts from short sentences to long, and the variety of sentence forms.

But rhythm is also fashioned by the sense. Good writers and speakers have an ear for matching the two. The best way to achieve good rhythms is to listen to those of good writers and speakers. Hear the rhythms of good writers as you read, read their paragraphs aloud and notice how easy they are to read, how each paragraph tends to build up to its own distinctive rhythm.

Notice how Dickens varies his rhythms between harmonious and disharmonious scenes. He would pace his study reading his work to make sure it was speakable – and not only the dialogue. Read the best playwrights, especially if it's conversational and speech-making skills you're keen to improve. Hear the characters' speeches in your head and read them aloud too, as their creators did to test whether they were speakable.

Rhythm and emphasis

The key to a satisfying rhythm is in **repetition**: of sounds (assonance and alliteration), of words and phrases, and of forms. The rhythm as well as the order of words in a sentence establishes where the emphases lie. Consider these sentences from V. S. Naipaul's essay 'The Return of Eva Peron', from his book with that title, describing a government building in Buenos Aires:

> There is beauty still in the spiked wall, the tall iron gates, the huge wooden doors. But inside, the walls peel; the windows in the central patio are broken; farther in, courtyard opening into courtyard, washing hangs in a corridor, steps are broken, and a metal spiral staircase is blocked with junk. This is a government office, a department of the Ministry of Labour: it speaks of an administration that has seized up, a city that is dying, a country that hasn't really worked.

Notice the different effects on rhythm, pace and emphasis of the commas, semi-colons, colon and full stops. Notice also how emphasis is given to the *beginnings* or *endings* of the sentences (or to both), and how the repetition of the *forms* of the final clauses create a rhythm that makes both subjects and verbs resound.

This kind of parallelism can make the most abstract of sentences forceful. Consider this sentence from a sociological essay on education by Basil Bernstein:

> Organic solidarity refers to social integration at the level of individualized, specialized, interdependent social roles whereas mechanical solidarity refers to social integration at the level of shared beliefs.

There is much repetition, but you welcome the way the rhythm created makes for clarity.

Practice

1. Rewrite the following sentences, which came from students' essays, more forcefully:

   (a) It is true to say that a great deal of the

bad behaviour we see around us today is caused by a lack of purposefulness in life.

(b) A major contribution to the creation of ugliness in our towns at this moment in time is the number of empty shops piled with litter and other rubbish.

(c) At various points in the novel various details of the street in which the policeman lives are included for the purpose of creating an eerie atmosphere, he includes them in order to make the reader feel something sinister is about to happen.

(d) When Laertes has finished a long sermon-like speech to his sister Ophelia on the bad results that could ensue from being too flirty, she gives her brother an answer which is full of good-humoured irony.

2. Rewrite the following paragraph, improving the rhythm and links, and achieving better emphases with the word order. Make sure you have fewer changes of subject.

The deciphering of the book of human life

– the genome – has just been finished by scientists, who have produced a DNA blueprint which will change everything. This knowledge was not considered possible to acquire until quite recently, but it has already begun to alter agriculture, forensic science, archaeology, biology and medicine. New multi-billion pound industries will be based on the software of life, driven by this new knowledge, for the years of the future. Human health will begin to be improved and human health will begin to be prolonged. It could begin to dictate the future, and the lives of the as-yet-unborn could begin to be shaped.

5 Winning Your Audience

*Using words effectively means communicating
what you mean to an audience whose attention is
firmly engaged.*

Is this you?

I was asked by the Senior Manager to find out
what caused an accident in the machine room
which injured two operators. I wrote him a
memo that concluded: 'It is incontrovertible
that the cause of the accident was the non-
availability of prompt assistance in the form
of an experienced supervisor.' The manager
said, 'Do you mean the supervisor wasn't
there?' I was compelled to allow that
interpretation – I mean I said yes. Especially
at work I tend to talk and write in a
pretentious way. I suppose it's because I'm
trying to appear knowledgeable. Also some
senior executives talk like that and I get it
from them.

Speaking what you've written

If you wonder whether something you've written is too full of abstractions, or too pretentious, or appears to be trying to hide something or to mislead, put 'Jack' or 'Susan' into the middle of it and see if you can say it. Would you say, 'It is incontrovertible, Jack...'?*

Winning your audience means meeting their needs. Consider your audience's age range, educational level, level of knowledge in your subject, and level of interest in it. What sort of language will grab and hold their attention? What terms will need explaining? A mainly formal or informal approach? Make it clear what your viewpoint is, to help your audience decide where they stand in relation to your subject.

You can win your audience by:

1. grabbing the attention

2. telling the truth

3. finding the right field

4. choosing the right register

* First, have something to say. Second, decide who you're saying it to. Third, communicate it in the most effective way.

5. establishing your point of view.

Grabbing the attention

To attract the attention of someone you're passing on the other side of the street you'll have to do something fairly striking: wave or shout, or both. It's obvious that you won't say 'hello' in your normal voice or begin an abstruse argument about the significance of Plato's teachings today. They will walk past without noticing.

The audience for a speaker or a piece of writing are cold, 'on the other side of the street', and you may have only a vague idea of who they are. Find out, therefore, before you address them, as much as you can about them. Then work out a more subtle and more binding form of shouting and waving to warm them up, attract and engage their attention. It must be assumed that you are greatly enthused by your subject and that you want to communicate that enthusiasm.

Leave deep and complex thoughts, if they are part of what you have to say, till later. For most subjects, if you start with abstract material, your audience will switch off. Lead your audience from concrete to abstract, from the familiar to the unfamiliar. Devices include an example, an analogy (as I have done at the start of this section), an anecdote, a quote, a quotation, a joke and a figure of speech. But make sure that start-off material is relevant and integrated, and that your subject is briskly introduced.

The same devices may be drawn on, with the same caveat, at any later stage of your communication and are discussed further in Chapters 6 and 7.

Telling the truth

Telling the whole truth should be your aim, as far as possible, given the time at your disposal and the circumstances. You may not know all the facts and it may not be possible to gather all the facts, but give significant ones, and aim to avoid vagueness.

If you know that the racial conflict started up between Albanians and Pakistanis, say so, rather than 'between certain ethnic groups'. Don't say the event began 'in mid-afternoon' if you know it was three o'clock.

Watch out for ambiguities

Ambiguities indicate that you have not paid close attention to the facts, and have not done enough thinking about your subject. It is easy to be ambiguous in English because of the varied interpretations a word may possess. A pharmacist would be unwise to say 'We dispense with accuracy'.

Carelessness in the choice of your words can have dire consequences. It turned out that a man accused in court of 'threatening to drive his next-door neighbour from her house' was offering her a lift to the shops.

Finding the right field

Look up the word *gate* in your dictionary and see how the meaning varies depending on the subject field (in front of a house, at an airport, an electric circuit, and so on). Look up the word *ground*, and note the same sort of changes, and also the various idiomatic phrases it gives rise to.

By *tragic* you may mean 'disastrous' if you're engaged in everyday language, but if you're classifying a work of literature the word means something much more specific. *Depression* has one meaning in geology and another in psychology.

Dictionaries now give several **regional variations**. Take the word *factor*. As well as distinct meanings for the fields of biology, mathematics, physiology and business, there is the meaning of land agent or steward, 'chiefly Scottish'. Other regional meanings relate to the USA, Canada, India and Australia.

Use the needed jargon

The word *gate* (meaning electric circuit) is an example of technical jargon (words or expressions used by a particular profession or group that are difficult for others to understand). You have to define such words unless you're addressing the group to whom they are familiar. If you're addressing non-lawyers you would have to explain the jargon of 'contempt', 'plead' and 'prejudice' to distinguish it from the everyday meanings of the words. Talking about literature, 'romantic' and 'tragic' as genre terms have to be distinguished from their general meaning.*

Choosing the right register

'Register' refers to 'a variety of a language determined by a degree of formality and choice of vocabulary, pronunciation and syntax'. In other words, 'level of usage'. Is the register *archaic*, *colloquial*, *formal*, *informal*, *obscene*, *obsolescent*, *offensive*, *old-fashioned*, *slang*, *vulgar*?

Consider the way *square* and *cool* are used to describe behaviour. The *Concise Oxford Dictionary* gives the meanings under the register label of *informal*: respectively, 'a person considered to be old-fashioned or boringly conventional', and 'fashionably attractive or impressive...excellent'. Such words may have a short life or may become firmly established. At the time of writing, *square* with the informal meaning has

* *Bureaucratic jargon was stigmatised as gobbledygook in Chapter 4.*

dropped out and *cool* is (perhaps) being worked to death.

Establishing your point of view

An undergraduate essay on philosophy is likely to be *impersonal,* whereas a talk to children in your local library about your visit to a pygmy tribe in Africa will be *personal.* Once your point of view is established, probably in your first paragraph, maintain it consistently, with not too many shifts to another.

In how-to writing, like this book, the point of view is personal but with the focus on *you* rather than *I*. If a how-to text sounds hectoring or too pedantic, sprinkle one or two impersonal passives in. For example, 'it's a good idea to . . . ', 'it's wise to . . . ', 'it might be worth . . . '.

In writing as well as speaking, your audience is attracted or put off by your **tone of voice**. The clearer your picture of your audience, the easier it will be to make your tone appropriate. Especially when you have serious matters to discuss, it is easy to be pompous, preachy or hectoring without being aware of it. Compare the buttonholing tone of the tabloid newspapers to the more intellectual tone of the broadsheets, so very different yet each entirely appropriate to their readerships. Obviously enough, listen to a speech in your head or read it aloud to yourself or to a friend or colleague to hear how it *sounds*; but do this also for any piece of writing you do. Alternatively, use a tape recorder.

Practice

1. Rewrite the following gobbledygook in not more than 90 words. Make sure it is user-friendly and improve the order.

   I should make it absolutely clear to you as an employee of this company that the enclosed questionnaire has been designed as a means of consultation with employees with respect to any recommendations or objections to the proposed reorganisation of the department in the form of teams with carefully defined responsibilities as discussed at our recent monthly meetings. There is no doubt in my mind that such a procedure will result in employees having the capacity to prioritise their workloads to the benefit of greater efficiency all round. It has come to my notice that certain employees have expressed reservations as to the desirability or feasibility of reorganisation of the department as set out in the proposal. Please be aware that completion of the enclosed questionnaire will enable such employees to make their recommendations and/or objections in specific terms. It is axiomatic that points made in completed forms will gain pre-eminence over any arguments presented at a later date. (160 words)

2. Write six sentences, each containing the word *head* in a different field meaning.

6 Finding the Right Words

The right word is the precise word. It communicates exactly what you mean. It's not usually the most impressive word, nor the most unusual, though it may take longer to find.

Ernest Hemingway, the American writer, when asked why he wrote dozens of drafts of the final page of his novel *Farewell to Arms* before he was satisfied, said 'To get the words right'. To write well you need to have this professional approach: amateurs may be easily pleased with their first or second draft and surprised when readers are much less pleased. Keeping to correct grammar and usage, for example, is a matter of showing your audience respect. You don't set out from your home in the morning in your pyjamas.

Spend as much time as you can spare on your drafts, taking pains to find those right words, using dictionary and thesaurus so that your active vocabulary increases in tandem with your passive one.

Meanwhile, this chapter provides some guidelines that will help your progress. You can find the right words by:

1. respecting good grammar

2. following accepted usage

3. sorting out the confusables

4. preferring concrete to abstract

5. aiming at precision.

Is this you?

Far too many people in my opinion go on and on about correct grammar, know what I mean? Its some time since I been in like, full time education and I want to get back into it to do a degree course in Sociolagy and there are would you believe people tellin me, I ought to have some privet lessons in English prior even to, thinkin about it. I believe in what my English teacher told me at school when they had the write ideas about these things when she said you do'nt wanto weigh yourself down with rigid grammar becos it gets, in the way of creativness where as now its all leage tables and dotin your is and crossing your tees. I can read the *Daily Mail* or most've it's content in a couple of hours which up until recently I couldnt do that. If you get my drift.

Respecting good grammar

Many languages have rigid grammar rules. English grammar, as a subject of study, is strictly speaking a set of rules (however tentatively they may sometimes be applied) about *syntax* (the arrangement of words and phrases in well-formed sentences) and *morphology* (the inflections and other forms of words). In practice grammar is taken to include rules or guidance on matters of vocabulary (technically called *lexis*), spelling, punctuation, usage, word order and idiom. Computer programs called grammar checks generally cover these aspects, except for spelling which is covered by spell checks.

Both checks have limitations, which can be

labelled the 'blind idiot' syndrome. This characteristic is illustrated by the story of the computer trying to translate 'out of sight, out of mind' and prescribing (when you translated it back) 'blind idiot'. Another computer condemned Lincoln's Gettysburg address (widely regarded as one of the greatest examples of speech-making) with a score of 0. Faults detected included 'too many passives, weak phrases and verbosity'.

Current grammar-check programs should be used with caution: though they're getting better they won't recognise your outstanding originality. There are many up-to-date books on grammar and usage that are worth having for reference if you want greater coverage of these subjects than you find in your dictionary. They are not, on the whole, prescriptive in the old style, Good English is clear, they emphasise, bad English is unclear.

Common instances of ungrammatical English are:

~ misplaced participles

~ ambiguous use of personal pronouns

~ abuse of relative pronouns.

Misplaced participle: 'Having served five years in prison for forgery, I am of the opinion that Malcolm Brown should not be considered for the job.' Is it 'I' or Malcolm Brown who has been in prison?

Ambiguous use of personal pronoun: 'It is natural to feel resentment towards your child. Get rid of *it* as soon as you can.' The resentment or the child?

Abuse of relative pronouns 1: 'I talked to Mrs Jones, *whom* I knew was leaving by train.' Replace *whom* with *who:* the relative pronoun is the subject of 'was leaving', not the object of 'knew'.

Abuse of relative pronouns 2: I can read the *Daily Mail* or most of it in a couple of hours, *which* until recently I couldn't do *that.* Delete *that:* the relative pronoun replaces it.

Following accepted usage

Here are four areas where uncertainties can gather:

Connotations

The dictionary says: 'an idea or feeling which a word invokes in addition to its primary meaning'. The connotations of a word may vary according to the company it keeps. Consider the difference between a *plausible rogue* and a *plausible theory*. The adjective means 'believable' in both cases, but to the first phrase accrues the idea of regret or suspicion.

Other Englishes

An American current affairs analyst for the BBC World Service was told by a BBC producer that his pronunciation of *schedule* was incorrect.

'The "sh" sound in *schedule* comes from German,' the producer said, 'as in *Schulz* or *Schnitzel*. It is not a "k" sound.'

'I suppose you learned that in shule,' the American said. To keep the peace he said 'timetable'.

Britain is justly proud of having fostered one of the world's greatest languages. But it is now a global language used by many people all over the world, who number many times over the UK population. A condescending attitude to regional variations speaks only of ignorance.

Sexist language

The use of male nouns and pronouns when the content refers to both sexes is an old habit still in evidence.

Example: 'If a customer complains, he is immediately given access to the manager.'

'He/she' or 's/he' are awkward solutions. More useful devices are:

Use the passive: '...immediate access is given to the manager.'

Use the plural: 'If customers complain, they are....'

Examples: 'Man's achievements', 'the average man', 'manpower'.

Rewrite: 'human achievements', 'the average person, 'the workforce'.

Political correctness

Sexist language is 'politically incorrect' or 'non-PC'. Various ways of referring to minorities are non-PC. Accepted or PC terms are: Blacks, the disabled (not 'crippled', to which the dictionary gives the registers *archaic* or *offensive*), Down's syndrome children (not 'Mongoloid' – *offensive*), and so on. Much work has been done to remove offensive terms from literature and to persuade people to follow guidelines set by local governments and other organisations, especially in the public sector.

Political correctness can, however, be carried to absurd lengths, to where the strictures can cause more harm than good. The following cases, I believe, fall into this category:

~ Police officers, it is reported, have been given a dictionary of language that must be avoided. Among expressions banned is 'rule of thumb', because it once referred to the width of a stick with which a man was allowed to beat his wife.

~ It used to be called *crowd control*. Nowadays you're more likely to see it referred to as *Visitor Flow Management*.*

* *Fun can be had with euphemisms masquerading as PC forms:* follically challenged *for* bald, altitudinally challenged *for* short, *etc.*

Sorting out the confusables

Homonyms are words having the same spelling or sound as others, but with different meanings, and are easily confused. Those with the same spelling are also called *homographs*. There are, for example, *pole* – a slender rounded piece of wood and metal; and *pole* – as in North Pole.

Homonyms with the same sounds but different spellings are called *homophones* (for example, *there*, *their*, and *they're*).

Another group of confusables are words similar in spelling: *mitigate/militate*, *composed/comprised*, *complement/compliment*, *sensual/sensuous*.

Preferring concrete to abstract

Use the concrete rather than the abstract, talk about people rather than theories. Use figurative language to make your audience see, hear, smell, touch, taste, as appropriate. However abstract your discourse has to be, it is usually possible to add pictures to it, or to translate into pictures. Here are some guidelines:

Say it concretely

To bring the abstract to life, use **examples**, **analogies**, **illustrations** and **anecdotes** to bring the abstract to life.

If you want to discuss the popular misconceptions about the risks we face in daily life, you'll be much more convincing if you have some reliable **statistics**. According to a recent report (the figures will need updating) heart diseases are twice as common as cancer, not the reverse; a car driver is 18 times more likely to die in a crash than a train passenger.

Attempts to describe fall flat without **specifics**: 'there were beautiful flowers in vases in various parts of the room' is much inferior to an account of which flowers, what colours, what shapes, what colours and shapes of vases, which parts of the room, and so on. Avoid such vague adjectives as *beautiful*, *splendid*, *marvellous* in writing, and don't overuse them in speech if you want people to listen to what you're saying.

Occasionally, when you can't find your own precise words, use quotations. If they are well known, you can get away with not using quotation marks. You won't need them for 'damn with faint praise' or 'willing to wound and yet afraid to strike': both from the eighteenth-century poet Alexander Pope, both clichés they are used so often, but if these things are what you want to say, is it possible to say them better?

Say it with people

Help your audience to identify with your subject by relating it to people. When preparing a substantial piece, the newspaper reporter's 'Five Ws Plus How' formula (Who, What, Where, When, Why and How) is a useful brainstorming technique. Suppose you are writing on 'How far does TV affect our relationships?' You might want to outline it round the following questions:

~ **Who?** The family viewing patterns and the effects on relationships. Differences depending on age groups. Children, teenagers, adults, the elderly. Within a marriage, within a family, outside the family (school, work, other friends).

~ **What?** What kinds of content and treatment have beneficial effects? Educational, social problems, etc. What kinds have harmful effects? Sex and violence, etc.

~ **Where?** TV at home: one TV for the household, compared with several. Advantages and disadvantages in terms of relationships. TV at school/work.

~ **When?** Effects of moderate TV watching compared with excessive. Family meeting up for meals with conversation or mealtimes with telly. Has it 'destroyed the art of conversation'?

~ **Why?** Explain in what ways TV helps or hinders relationships, if not covered. Perhaps in psychological terms. Sum up on process.

~ **How?** Perhaps by illustrating the process by means of a **case study** or **anecdotes**.

Aiming at precision

The great wealth and resourcefulness of English, with its numerous synonyms and stylistic choices, can inspire us to use it with both imagination and precision. Consider the sets of synonyms from different origins. Old English *ask*, French *question*, Latin *interrogate*, for example, allow us to choose among ordinary, more formal and more restricted (e.g. professional) usage.

Such sets are numerous. The resourcefulness can, of course, when concentration flags or pomposity intervenes, encourage (to all intents and purposes what can be described as) verbosity. Remove what's in that long bracket, I hear you cry. Precisely!

Practice

1. Write sentences containing each of the following pairs of words in order to distinguish them. Then check your dictionary to see if you have distinguished them correctly:

official/officious
contemptuous/contemptible
credible/credulous
judicial/judicious

2. The following sentences are incorrect or ambiguous. Rewrite, then check with the key on page 122.

(a) The soldier as well as his brothers are clearly annoyed by the hostility of the neighbours.

(b) Parliament has adjourned for their summer recess.

(c) The criteria for judging it to be a good piece of work is in a list compiled by the manager.

(d) Whom do you consider is the best player in the team?

(e) As someone whose had a lot of experience of organising parties, there is no better place for one.

(f) They could have attempted to have informed the police yesterday.

(g) The Brown's may have gone on holiday if their passports had arrived on time.

(h) No persons who have not filled in a form will be eligible for this excursion, but will be able to apply for the next one.

(i) I'm surprised that you associate with these sort of layabouts.

(j) Your pets obviously like me more than you.

3. Pick out the errors in the **Is this you?** section on page 75.

7 Being Original

It's not only the words you choose that count but where you put them, and then it is having the confidence to say things in your own way.

Being original means, essentially, being yourself, individual in what you have to say and in the way in which you say it: individual in **content** and **style**.

The lecturer may be the foremost expert on the subject and the lecture may contain exactly the content you need to know, but if the lecture is delivered in a toneless voice with little attention to arousing interest by rhythm, pace, varied emphases, and examples of a kind that bring the subject to life – all those qualities we call style – you may not stay awake long enough to learn. A written piece needs the same qualities to achieve impact.

Conversely, there is nothing more groan-making than style without substance in the content: a speech-maker or writer full of personality but little else. It is originality in what you have to say that will call for originality in your words and their arrangements. Learn by listening to good speakers and reading good writers. You may find it useful to tape-record a compelling speaker or broadcast and to photocopy published pieces that grab you. Make notes.

Though for convenience you will analyse content and style separately, you will notice that they go together like body and soul, and that in the best speakers and writers you will not see any straining for effect. But keep in mind that their success may be the result of great commitment and much practice.

Become original by:

1. avoiding clichés

2. appealing to the senses

3. using other literary techniques

4. developing your own style.

Is this you?

I used to be the life and soul of the party
with my anecdotes. It was the way I told 'em,
they said, and I had a way with written words
as well until people started saying I'm always
using clichés and not expressing myself in my
own way. If that's the way the cookie
crumbles I've got to nip it in the bud and get
up to speed. The trouble is, I spend an
inordinate amount of time trying to produce
a user-friendly style, but at the end of the day
it's all hit and miss, and it becomes
increasingly apparent that I've got to change
my spots. Mind you, I'm a mine of
information about all kinds of subjects and
mutatis mutandis I'll have to learn how to
hack it, otherwise they'll be saying I was just
the flavour of the month.

Avoiding clichés

A cliché is a hackneyed or overused phrase or
opinion. Clichés are overused because they
are so readily available among the furniture of
our minds. They can be trotted out to save us

the trouble of expressing something in a fresh way, which takes more effort.

They have their attractions and their uses. Some date from centuries ago and still retain some impact. It was in 1546 that John Heywood said he knew *what side his bread was buttered on*. At least you can appreciate how fresh it was at the time. Clichés can quickly attract attention at the start of a greeting or conversation, and help to create an easy farewell, the verbal equivalents of waves of recognition and of goodbye to a friend seen across the street. Their familiarity can help you make a quick friend of listener or reader. If your essay or article or whatever is complex or profound, a cliché can give the reader a welcome breather.

Having said that, use them gratefully, not patronisingly, when you have to, without describing quotation marks in the air. That is trying to have it both ways. And use them sparingly, especially in writing.

There are various kinds of cliché: overworked phrases, with vogue words or foreign words, stock modifiers and misused colloquialisms are among the most common.

~ Watch out for such **overworked phrases** with **vogue words** as: *a no-win situation, the bottom line, a typical scenario, in the current climate,* and the **foreign** ones that are either unnecessary (*au fond* for 'basically') or perhaps seen too often (*tête-à-tête*).

~ **Stock modifiers** have a bad habit of barging their way into your communications: *visibly moved, brownie points, woefully inadequate,* and so on. They are even less welcome when they come in alliterative pairs: *calm and collected, mean and moody*.

~ **Colloquialisms**, words used in ordinary conversation that are not formal nor literary, can become vogue and vague, with the original meaning weakened. Examples are *amazing, awesome, chronic, dire, magic* (as an adjective), *unreal, wicked*. Make sure you are getting the value you want from them; if not, find another word.

Appealing to the senses

Prefer concrete to abstract was advised in Chapter 6. Go further and use **figurative**, or metaphorical, language, departing from a literal use of words, when you want to inspire, be vivid, be poetic, rise above the ordinary. Read the great writers, particularly poets, to see how it can be done. Quote well-known lines of poetry occasionally: with their resonance they can add richness or depth to what you're saying, but don't use those that are too well known, and use them very sparingly. Find your own metaphors.

Can Shakespeare be excused for those **mixed metaphors**, for Hamlet saying '...take arms against a sea of troubles...'? You decide. What's certain is that you won't be excused for saying that someone's argument is 'in a nutshell, a fine kettle of fish that doesn't stand up to scrutiny'.

Using other literary techniques

Among other literary techniques, **irony** (saying the opposite of what you mean, usually for humorous or satirical effect) and **humour** can lift your message and make it memorable. Audiences can leave a theatrical performance with one or two lines that they will never forget ringing in their ears: lines that either moved them deepest or made them laugh loudest.

English lends itself to all kinds of word play that makes a point ironically or humorously or both, and (with luck) memorably. Here are a few examples:

~ **Intentional ambiguity** (*amphibology*): 'Parents with complaints about the atrocious manners of the boys of this school should see the headmaster.'

~ **Irony:** 'So are they all, all honourable men' (Shakespeare's Mark Antony on those who assassinated Julius Caesar). In milder mode, irony can be conveyed by using **euphemisms**: newspapers can refer to a politician being drunk and avoid being sued for libel by referring to their being 'tired and emotional'. Using quotation marks can make it clear (if it's not obvious) that the words don't mean exactly what they say.

~ **Surprise:** 'You must remember that under that cold exterior beats a heart of stone.' This is a kind of irony, in that expectations are reversed.

~ **Puns:** Don't groan too much at the puns that come with the conundrums that children ply you with, since they are a start to getting fun and profit from word play. *Example*: If you stumble over your new mat in the passage, what science are you shown to have neglected? *Pneumatics*.

A good pun can give a flash of insight or say something worth saying memorably. Two good ones, I think, are:

'The neighbours were arguing from different premises.'
'We must all hang together or assuredly we shall all hang separately.' (Benjamin Franklin, eighteenth-century American statesman, encouraging his fellow-countrymen during the War of Independence with Britain.)

Developing your own style

Bad style is straining for effect. A story about ancient Egypt begins:

> I was idly noticing the negligible effect of the *adan* upon the occupants of the neighbouring shops when suddenly my errant attention became arrested. A mendicant of unwholesome aspect crouched in the shadow of the narrow gateway.

The essence of good style is that it is **natural.** Natural for you, for what you have to say, for who you're talking to. You may have to vary your style for different audiences, but it remains natural.

In straightforward prose, as in the best journalism, it may be hardly noticed. The writer has a fair idea of who the readers are and, like Christina Odone on page 35, is talking clearly and directly to them. More complex or more profound subject matter demands a more complex style, but the criterion is: is it as clear and readable as that subject matter allows? The sociological

sentence on page 61 illustrated how **rhythm**
and **parallelism** can help when your terms
have to be abstract.

Other techniques may be demanded by a
more colourful subject matter. To give the
reader a jolt you may need to milk the more
striking of the devices mentioned in this
chapter, learnt rather than borrowed from
good writers – startling figurative language,
sudden changes of pace, dramatic emphases.
But it should still be hard to separate the *how*
from the *what*.

If you're engaged in creative writing you
may be less concerned with the audience and
more concerned to experiment with language,
to use words and arrange them in unusual
ways as you explore new territory. But you
will still be concerned to be understood, in
what is recognisably your way.

Practice

1. Complete the following clichés, and then
   try not to use them again:
   (a) dicing with . . . , (b) calm before the . . . ,

(c) run of the..., (d) bone of..., e) a hand to mouth..., (f) a level..., (g)...will tell, (h)...the stops, (i)...truth, (j)...aforethought, (k)...of discontent.

2. Rewrite in three sentences and, in a more lively and more personal style, this notice posted on a library notice board:

Important Notice to Local Parents:
In the event of the schools in this area being liable to closure for a number of days as a result of the necessity to deal with flood damage, the events we have prepared to meet that contingency and propose to be held in the Central Library, providing educational and entertaining activities for primary school children for the duration of such a period are expected to be acknowledged with a considerable degree of pleasure by parents. Their concern at the prospect of enforced idleness for their children is understandably considerable, and any suggestions as to the form the proposed events might take will be given due consideration, provided the

costs would be commensurate with our budget capabilities. Suggestions may be made on the forms supplied and inserted in the Suggestions Box.

Head Librarian

8 Speaking to Greater Effect

*'Know thyself', be curious to know others, and
have a desire to communicate with them: these
are the makings of a good speaker.*

They say that the art of conversation is dead, killed by TV sets and home computer games in every room, and TV mealtimes. They say that rather than sitting down to chat with friends face to face we have forgotten what they look like because we are either all alone sending out emails or jabbering away on mobiles giving unnecessary even if brief briefings whenever there is a minute or two to spare ('I'm on the bus...'). The doomsters are exaggerating, of course. Nevertheless, there is no doubt that much of new technology exalts the image over the word and that speaking skills are in decline.

Parliament used to be full of great orators. It was always noisy, but the noises used to be well worth listening to. Schoolchildren used to learn poetry by heart, and how to recite it well. The cadences influenced their speech, and the pleasure of possessing words remained with them throughout their lives. No longer. All sad and true. On the other hand, both speakers and writers have to adapt to the world they're living in, not cling to the world that has gone, and there are virtues in the way we can now get quickly to the point and in our distrust of rhetoric for its own sake. You can achieve superior sound bites, however, by:

1. improving your conversation

2. preparing your speech

3. applying voice power.

Improving your conversation

From casual conversations with a friend, through dinner party discussions, informal talks, class discussions, seminars, lectures and set speeches, you are challenged to adapt to a world of language changing as rapidly as all the other worlds we inhabit. Whatever your particular needs and goals, you can start by improving that casual conversation, for the essential qualities of good conversation are those of good speech making and good writing.

When you think about what goes wrong when people lack verbal communication skills, you realise there's nothing new about it. Relationships break up because those in them don't know how to speak to each other, people being interviewed for a job are turned down because they can't express themselves effectively, employers don't work effectively because their employees don't know how to give instructions clearly, and peoples go to war because they don't know how to exchange ideas. Since the basis of language is the spoken word, if we can't speak effectively we probably can't write effectively either.

Where to start? Socrates' '**Know thyself**' means deciding where you fit into the scheme of things, what your relationship is to ofthers, what you can contribute to the community (all right, the world) you belong to. **Know others** means liking them (on the whole) and being curious about them, aiming to understand yourself through them and understand them through yourself. **The desire to communicate** is an essential part of the human condition, and the more enjoyment and enthusiasm you have in communicating, the more effective your communication is likely to be.

The most common turn-off, for whatever size of audience, is speakers who are full of themselves, even when there is plenty to be full of. You must address the needs of the audience. When you're not getting across, your friend may tactfully tell you that you're being boring, a schoolroom may become restless, an audience for a speech may have a shipwrecked, waiting-to-be-rescued look. The signs of disaffection may be more subtle, but you will soon learn to recognise them.

Is this you?

Even conversing with friends I can get nervous, and my voice becomes high pitched and I find they're not listening to what I'm saying. • If I have to deliver a speech I make notes as I would for an essay, then I write it out on A4 sheets. The main points are headings in red ink at the top of a page. • I memorise the main points with the idea that I won't have to *read*. I keep the script in front of me as security, expanding on the main points that I have in my head, referring to the script only to jog my memory. • That's the theory. In practice I get nervous, the words don't flow, and I often end up reading every word. • I can't seem to maintain eye contact with the audience and read at the same time, and I tend to forget to vary my tone of voice as well in my anxiety to get to the end. The whole thing can become quite boring. • Once a draught from an open window blew away the pages of my script. A member of the audience gathered them up, while I stood there trying to keep going. Not successfully. I'd forgotten the exact order of those points. • The pages weren't numbered, and it took me a couple of minutes (or was it a couple of hours?) to put them in order. My voice now had an alarming strangled-sounding tone and my swallowing large gulps of air only compounded the problem. • Even when there are no disasters of such obvious kinds, and I have worked out a good shape for a speech, and it's a subject that fascinates me, I don't find it easy to share that fascination. It's usually because I haven't taken enough care to formulate the questions that will be in my audience's mind. And tried to answer them.

Preparing your speech

Bring the content to life

Since the audience for your speech cannot go back and remind themselves what you've said, you generally have to treat your subject matter in a more lively and memorable way than you would if you were writing it. That may mean more attention to moving from abstract to concrete, to saying it with people, to using humour, anecdotes and figurative language. It will certainly mean repetition in such surprising or welcome ways that it won't produce boredom.

Get feedback

When preparing your speech, try out your ideas in conversation, get feedback and learn from it. When making your speech, even when your audience is silent, you can see their reactions in their body language and facial expressions. Learn to look for such reactions even in a large audience.

Plan

For a speech as for a piece of writing of any length, you will need to **outline your main points in the best order**. You may even want to write out the speech and learn it by heart. It is best, however, to allow for 'thinking on your feet' to some extent: following the prepared piece too rigidly is going to sound stilted, even if you write in the natural-sounding colloquial links listed below. Reading a speech word for word with little eye contact is likely to be disastrous.*

Use note cards

If you write out your speech, it is probably best to read it over several times so that you

* However well prepared a speech is, it must be **talked**.

know it very well, and at the time of delivery use 6″ × 4″ catalogue cards, or make your own, in thin cardboard, numbered for order. Don't use paper which will rustle, especially if you're using a microphone: it will pick up the noise. Each card should have a heading in capitals followed by brief notes – enough to enable you to expand fluently. Write notes large enough to be seen at stomach height.

Glancing at the card should be sufficient to take you through the aspect covered, at the same time **maintaining eye contact** with your audience. Don't continue an aspect of your subject onto another card. There will be a natural pause as you move from one card to the next. You may want to insert a link at the bottom of a card, or you may prefer to use whatever link comes to you at the time. Find one or two ways of signalling rhythm and pace. You may want to keep the cards together with a filing tag.

Rehearse it

Practise giving your speech a few times to make sure it is speakable. The best of written sentences may be difficult to speak well. Get more feedback from others if you can. You may want to record your speech on tape. When you play back the tape, you will be made more sharply aware of any voice problems, of any lack of rhythm and pace and of any lack of links.

Link up

The linking words and phrases mentioned in Chapter 2 will serve for speeches, but you may want to make them more informal. Here are a few suggestions:

Writing	Speech
For example	Say
Furthermore	Not only that
The result was	As it turned out
On the other hand	Yes but
Take the case	Tell you what
That may be the case	So what?

Applying voice power

Accentuate the positive

The need to speak in plummy or 'posh' public school accents in order to be taken seriously in Britain has gone. Standard English, Standard American and Standard Australian refer to standards of correct grammar, usage and pronunciation (not the same thing as accent). They vary, and are equally 'correct': the global character and great flexibility of the language prevent it from becoming strictly regulated.

If you have a strong regional accent, for areas and audiences that find it impenetrable you'll have to develop a clear, less regional one. Clarity will be assisted by sounding your consonants clearly. Don't copy a general tendency to slovenliness (as in *thinkin* for *thinking*), or the posh tendency to say *lor'norda* for *law and order* and to strangle vowels. Don't attempt to sound fashionably classless, noted especially among politicians and TV presenters, it results in flat, toneless sounds.

You may want to keep (or find it hard to

lose) your regional accent when you're among the people you grew up with. There's no reason for you to lose it at those times. Make sure you sound **natural** to the people you're addressing. If you aim at posh and sound affected you risk being ridiculed. The current drive to teach schoolchildren to speak (as well as write) better is welcome, but an undue emphasis on Standard English in the UK should be resisted. The wonderful richness of regional ways of speaking English – the dialects, the sounds, the rhythms – must be preserved. Just as the poetry reflecting that richness — of the Irish Yeats, the Scottish Burns, the Welsh Dylan Thomas, the North of England Ted Hughes, and of so many other regional English poets — must be preserved.

Make your tone of voice interested

We are back to the advice to *talk*, *don't read*. A monotonous voice will turn an audience off, an interested tone will help to grab its attention. Use the natural gestures and body language in general, including facial expressions, that go with your talking to friends. To help the audience to keep on the track, make sure the rhythm and pace you've signalled in the verbal content (see above) are realised in your speaking. Dramatically, when appropriate.

Get the timing right

Which brings us, last but not least, to **timing**. When to pause, when to roll on, when to pause briefly, when to make it long, when to be loud, when to be quiet, when to emphasise, when to throw away, when to repeat, when to digress, when to smile, when to frown. To learn timing watch actors and stand-up comedians as well as good speakers.

Timing involves knowing where to begin and where to end. This is the end of this book, because although there's a lot more to be said about word power it's time for you to say it in the way you use your growing stock of words.

Practice

Sir Winston Churchill gave a famous speech in

Parliament during the Second World War. After saying, 'You ask, what is our aim?' a part of his speech may be paraphrased as follows:

> There is a brief, monosyllabic answer to that and it is: Victory. I am of the firm opinion that we should bend all our efforts towards achieving a successful outcome to our struggle, whatever the cost may be to us in the end, and even if we have to conquer terror on the way, and no matter how long and difficult the road may be before we reach it, because we won't survive if we don't achieve it. We must realise these things, and that the British Empire will not survive, nor will all that the British Empire has represented.

Rewrite more memorably in 50–55 words.

Appendix: Key to tasks

Compare the following responses, which are not intended to be definitive, with your own. Yours may be better. Consult your dictionary for further enlightenment.

Chapter 1

1. (a) experienced indirectly
   (b) famous for something bad
   (c) concise
   (d) bitter
   (e) apparently true

2. (a) bibliophile
   (b) fixed
   (c) extraterrestrial
   (d) extraterritorial
   (e) nicety

3. (a) company
   (b) facetious
   (c) mutilate
   (d) similarity
   (e) misled

4. The *Concise Oxford* gives seven:
   (i) a circular piece or section

(ii) an act of visiting a number of people or places in turn, e.g. a newspaper round

(iii) each of a sequence of sessions in a process, especially in a sports contest

(iv) a song for three or more unaccompanied voices or parts, each singing the same theme but starting one after the other

(v) a set of drinks bought for all the members of a group, typically as part of a sequence in which each member in turn buys such a set

(vi) a slice of bread

(vii) the amount of ammunition needed to fire one shot.

5. sleeplessness

6. The main meanings of the words, the meanings that tend to be confused, are given. See your dictionary for other meanings.

(a) *catholic* means including a wide variety of things
Catholic means of the Roman Catholic faith

(b) *eligible* means satisfying the appropriate conditions
illegible means not clear enough to be read

(c) *cultured* means refined and well educated
cultivated can mean the same, or can refer to hand prepared for growing plants

(d) *sestet* means the last six lines of a sonnet
sextet means a group of six people playing music, a composition for them, or any group of six people

(e) *allusion* means an indirect or implicit reference
illusion means a false or unreal perception

(f) *credible* means able to be believed
credulous means being too ready to believe things

(g) *affect* means have an effect on, make a difference to
effect means cause to happen, bring about

(h) *imply* means indicate by suggestion
infer means deduce from evidence and reasoning rather than from explicit statements

(i) *pendant* means a piece of jewellery that hangs from a necklace chain
pendent means hanging down or pending (awaiting decision)

(j) *gourmand* means a person who enjoys eating, sometimes to excess
gourmet means a connoisseur of good food

Chapter 2

1. A patient with an unusual disease discovered on the internet a better treatment than that prescribed. He lost faith in his doctor, who had little experience of the disease. The patient realised that GPs couldn't keep up to date with the research on all the illnesses they were dealing with but he should have acknowledged that there is more to medicine than facts. Flushed with success

he continued to access internet help. When he contracted another disease he collected a mass of information, much of which was misleading, took two incompatible drugs together, and died. What he had lacked was the knowledge and judgement to assess the information. (108 words)

2. Opinions differ about whether England is now as class-ridden as it was, but it was undoubtedly a land of snobbery and privilege, and its rulers lacked vision. It is all the more surprising, then, to note that the English tend to unite at times of crisis, to close ranks and help each other, as they did during the two world wars.

Chapter 3

1. (a) The housing manager said that he would produce at the Thursday council meeting an updated computerised report on the repairs required.

   (b) The orchestra's performance was loudly appreciated.

(c) I was bored by the film we saw.
(d) The company was training staff to respond better to customers' complaints.

2. I'm now studying Computer Science, feeling that it will be useful whatever my career. I find that working long hours on the screen have not advanced my writing skills, although they seem to develop my ability to think laterally. I find it tedious to try to plan logically what I want to say, so I plunge into the writing and then rewrite if necessary. Unfortunately, once I see the draft it seems fine. (73 words)

Chapter 4

This task is based on the first paragraph of an article in *The Guardian* of 26 June 2000, which reads:

Scientists have just finished deciphering the genome – the book of human life. Their DNA blueprint will change everything. The once undreamed-of knowledge has already begun to alter agriculture, forensic

science, archaeology, biology and
medicine. In the next decades it will fuel
new multi-billion pound industries based
on the software of life. It will begin to
improve human health and prolong human
life. It could even begin to dictate the
future and shape the lives of the as-yet-
unborn. It will begin to alter – in the most
profound fashion – the way humans think
about themselves, and all life on the
planet.

Note on the paragraph to be rewritten

The paragraph on page 62 was hard to read
because of the changes in subject. 'It' in the
last sentence seems to refer to 'human health'
rather than to the 'knowledge'.

Notice the link words in the original
version above: *just*, *Their*, *already*, *next*, *even*.
The rhythms of the repetitions ('It will
begin . . . It could even begin . . . It will
begin . . . ') make things clearer. One or two of
the 'it's' could be replaced by 'that
knowledge' or 'the book' or 'the genome'.
What do you think?

2. (a) Many people behave badly today

because they lack purpose in life.
(b) The rubbish piled inside dismantled shops is now adding greatly to the ugliness of our towns.
(c) The author creates suspense in the novel with the sinister details of the street in which the policeman lives.
(d) Laertes warns Ophelia at length that her flirting is dangerous, and her answer is full of irony.

Chapter 5

1.

Reorganisation of the Department
I enclose a questionnaire to enable you to express your views on the above proposal. Please complete and return to me by the end of this week to make sure your views will be considered. I believe the recent monthly meetings held to discuss the proposed reorganisation of the department were useful and I want to thank all who participated. I'm sorry that some of you have doubts about the reorganisation. The main idea – teams with

carefully defined responsibilities – is surely worth exploring. (86 words including heading)

2. Six fields give you the following meanings for the word *head*:
   (a) anatomy: the part of the body
   (b) geography: the source of a river, the end of a lake
   (c) carpentry: the cutting end of a tool, the flattened end of a nail
   (d) botany: the compact mass of leaves or flowers at the top of a stem
   (e) education: the person in charge of an educational institution
   (f) certain liquids: the foam on top of a glass of beer, or the cream on top of milk.

If your sentences contain different meanings, check with your dictionary.

Chapter 6

2. Two versions are suggested for some sentences, and you may have produced yet another version, which could be correct.

(a) The soldier as well as his brothers is clearly annoyed by the hostility of the neighbours.

(b) Parliament have adjourned for their summer recess/Parliament has adjourned for its summer recess.

(c) The criterion for judging it to be a good piece of work is in a list compiled by the manager/The criteria . . . are . . .

(d) Who do you consider is the best player in the team?

(e) As someone who's had a lot of experience of organising parties, I say there is no better place for one/For me, as someone . . . parties, there is . . .

(f) They could have attempted to inform the police yesterday.

(g) The Browns might have gone on holiday if their passports had arrived on time.

(h) No new applicants for this excursion will be considered; all will have to fill in a form to apply for the next one.

(i) I'm surprised that you associate with these sorts of layabouts/ . . . with this sort of layabout.

(j) Your pets obviously like me more than they like you/ (or does it mean?): Your pets obviously like me more than you do.

3. Apart from one or two unnecessary words and phrases (like, *know what I mean*, *would you believe*), and the misplaced commas (can you spot them?), the corrections are:

(1) It's, (2) I've (been in), (3) Sociology, (4) telling, (5) private, (6) thinking, (7) right (ideas), (8) don't, (9) want to, (10) because, (11) creativeness, (12) whereas, (13) it's, (14) league, (15) dotting, (16) i's, (17) t's, (18) most of its (content), (19) which I couldn't do until recently.

Chapter 7

1. (a) dicing with death (b) calm before the storm (c) run of the mill (d) bone of contention (e) a hand to mouth existence (f) a level playing field (g) time will tell (h) pull out the stops (i) unvarnished truth (j) malice aforethought (k) winter of discontent.

2. If a notice is posted up on a board it must be important so there is no need to say 'Important Notice'. Give a notice a proper title:

IF SCHOOLS CLOSE...

...for some days because of the floods, we have planned educational and entertaining activities for primary school children at the Central Library. Any suggestions from anxious parents for activities that would be within our budget will be welcome. Please fill in the form supplied and insert in the Suggestions Box.

Head Librarian

Chapter 8

Churchill actually said:

I can answer in one word: Victory, victory at all costs, victory in spite of all terror, victory, however long and hard the road may be; for without victory, there is no survival. Let that be realised; no survival for the British Empire; no survival for all that the British Empire has stood for...
(54 words)